AND THEN THERE WERE NONE

A Comedy in One Act

by

R. F. DELDERFIELD

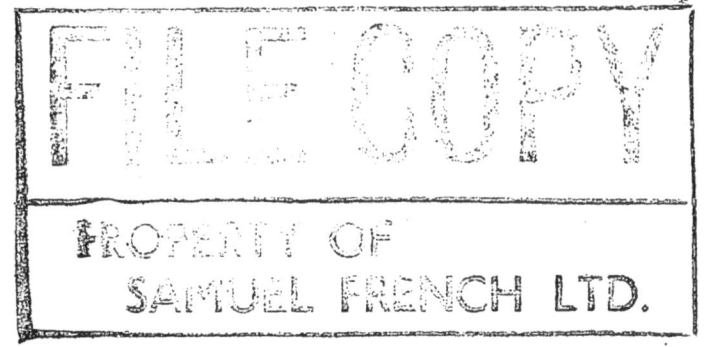

LONDON
SAMUEL FRENCH LIMITED

Copyright © 1954 by R.F. Delderfield
All Rights Reserved

AND THEN THERE WERE NONE is fully protected under the copyright laws of the British Commonwealth, including Canada, the United States of America, and all other countries of the Copyright Union. All rights, including professional and amateur stage productions, recitation, lecturing, public reading, motion picture, radio broadcasting, television and the rights of translation into foreign languages are strictly reserved.

ISBN 978-0-573-11460-1

www.samuelfrench.co.uk
www.samuelfrench.com

For Amateur Production Enquiries

United Kingdom and World excluding North America

plays@samuelfrench.co.uk

020 7255 4302/01

Each title is subject to availability from Samuel French, depending upon country of performance.

CAUTION: Professional and amateur producers are hereby warned that AND THEN THERE WERE NONE is subject to a licensing fee. Publication of this play does not imply availability for performance. Both amateurs and professionals considering a production are strongly advised to apply to the appropriate agent before starting rehearsals, advertising, or booking a theatre. A licensing fee must be paid whether the title is presented for charity or gain and whether or not admission is charged.

No one shall make any changes in this title for the purpose of production. No part of this book may be reproduced, stored in a retrieval system, or transmitted in any form, by any means, now known or yet to be invented, including mechanical, electronic, photocopying, recording, videotaping, or otherwise, without the prior written permission of the publisher. No one shall upload this title, or part of this title, to any social media websites.

The right of R.F. Delderfield to be identified as author of this work has been asserted by him in accordance with Section 77 of the Copyright, Designs and Patents Act 1988.

CHARACTERS

(in the order of their appearance)

SIR HECTOR FANSHAWE-SCOTT, Liberal M.P. for Blandford-cum-Gorton

THE RIGHT HONOURABLE ESMOND DELAHAYE, Sir Hector's secretary

TOPPING, the parlourmaid

THE SUFFRAGETTE

IRIS FANSHAWE-SCOTT, Sir Hector's only daughter

LADY FANSHAWE-SCOTT, Sir Hector's wife

The action of the play passes in an ante-room of the main drawing-room at Four Beeches, the large, suburban home of Sir Hector, on an evening during the General Elections of 1906

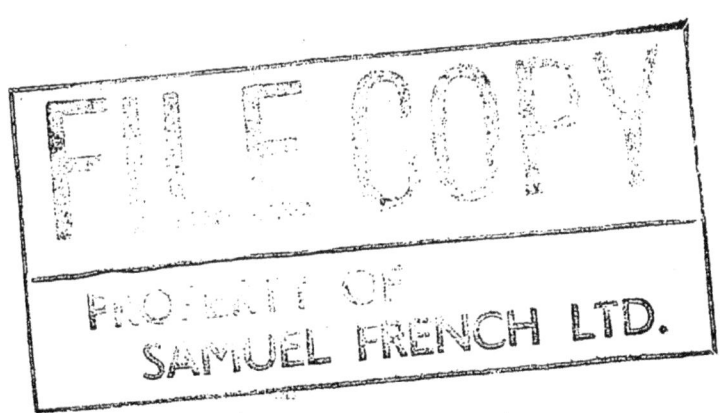

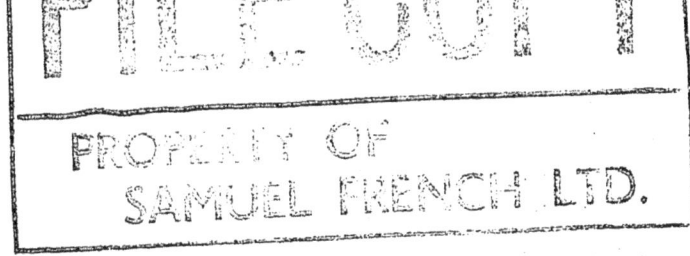

AND THEN THERE WERE NONE

Scene—*The ante-room of the main drawing-room at Four Beeches, the large, suburban home of Sir Hector. An evening during the General Elections of 1906.*

It is a small but comfortable room on the first floor of a large house in the outer suburb of an industrial city, and is used as an ante-room for Sir Hector, now using the main room as his local headquarters during the elections. There is a door up L *leading to the drawing-room and a door up* R *giving access to the landing and stairs. There is a small french window* C *of the back wall opening on to a balcony overlooking the garden. The mouthpiece of a speaking-tube protrudes from the wall below the door* R. *A table stands* RC. *It is set with a white cloth, plates, knives and a few dishes for a stand-up sandwich supper. There is a settee down* L, *and an armchair up* LC. *Upright chairs stand down* R, *up* R *and below the door* L. *Heavy curtains are looped back at the window. Other period furnishings may be added at the discretion of the Producer.*

(*See the Ground Plan at the end of the play*)

When the Curtain *rises, it is almost dark. The lamp on the table has been lit but the window curtains and window are open.* Sir Hector Fanshawe-Scott, *Liberal M.P. for Blandford-cum-Gorton, enters* R. *He is followed respectfully by his secretary,* The Right Honourable Esmond Delahaye. Sir Hector *is a self-important man, about fifty-five, a successful tradesman turned politician. At Westminster he has succeeded in having his good opinion of himself confirmed. He does not mean to be pompous and overbearing, for at heart he is a tolerant husband and a warm-hearted father, but his success has elevated him somewhat from his domestic surroundings and perhaps he is inclined to bluster in order to conceal humble origins. On the other hand,* Esmond *is public school, and blandly self-assured, whilst maintaining a very correct attitude towards his employer. He is a good-looking, con-*

ventional young man about twenty-five. *He has a notebook and pencil and is taking notes.*

SIR HECTOR (*crossing to* C) ... and then, in conclusion, I shall touch lightly—*lightly*, mind you—on Women's Suffrage. I don't intend to linger there. I shall simply make my attitude on the recent outrages abundantly clear.

ESMOND. I quite understand, sir. I'll check that part of your notes with the Press immediately after supper.

SIR HECTOR (*firmly*) By all means do. We don't want any misunderstanding as to where *my* sympathies lie in *that* particular direction.

ESMOND. And at what time precisely would you like Muspratt to unlock the main gates and let constituents into the garden, Sir Hector?

(SIR HECTOR *consults a large watch*)

SIR HECTOR. In about twenty minutes, but first we must check the main drift of my speech. I shall need the extra lighting on the balcony, of course.

ESMOND. I've arranged for it, sir, and light supper for the committee in here immediately you have acknowledged the ovation.

(TOPPING, *the trim parlourmaid, enters* R. *She is aged about twenty and carries some paper serviettes*)

SIR HECTOR. Naturally.

(TOPPING *moves to the table* RC)

Ah, Topping—don't let us run short of savouries again. Well-fed canvassers are conscientious canvassers, eh, Esmond?

ESMOND (*with a dutiful laugh*) Certainly, Sir Hector.

TOPPING. Her Ladyship told me, sir—I'm just bringing two extra plates of crab and relish.

ESMOND (*indicating the window up* C) Will you be using *this* balcony at all, Sir Hector?

SIR HECTOR. H'm—no, I think not, we don't want the electors looking in two places at once. My wife and daughter can squeeze in beside the agent and yourself on the drawing-room balcony. Come now, we shall need every second of this twenty minutes' grace.

(SIR HECTOR *crosses and exits purposefully* L)

ESMOND (*to* Topping) Draw those curtains and close the window, Topping.

TOPPING. Yes, sir. Certainly, sir.

(ESMOND *crosses and exits* L. TOPPING *does not immediately obey, but, with her back to the window, sets out the paper serviettes. Unseen by her there is a swift movement back* C.

The SUFFRAGETTE, *a young and attractive woman about twenty-two, slips in from the balcony and dives behind the bulge of curtains* L *of the window. She carries a basket and wears her outdoor clothes.* TOPPING *turns, moves to* R. *of the window, closes the right curtain, draws the window to, then reaches out to close the left curtain. With a strangled shriek she leaps back as the* SUFFRAGETTE *is revealed*)

Eowwwww!

(*The* SUFFRAGETTE, *by dramatic use of her voice and manner, compels a second's horrified silence*)

SUFFRAGETTE. Shhhh! Be silent!

(TOPPING *is still powerless to exclaim. Holding her heart, she collapses on to the settee. The* SUFFRAGETTE *dives across to the table and deposits her basket on it.* TOPPING *rises and runs towards the door* L, *but the* SUFFRAGETTE *is too quick for her. She catches* TOPPING *and hurls her back on to the settee*)

Don't move. And don't you dare to utter a sound.

(*Her resolution effectually quietens* TOPPING, *who continues to gaze at her in horror and amazement*)

I warn you. I'm desperate and—(*unconvincingly*) I'm—I'm armed. Where is the Member?

(TOPPING *mutely nods towards the door* L)

(*She tiptoes to the door* L, *listens, then, apparently satisfied, crosses to* C) That's all right. He's already intoxicating himself with his own platitudes. Tie up those curtains and open the window. Quickly! I don't want my retreat cut off.

(TOPPING *hurriedly rises, moves to the window, opens it and draws back the curtains*)

TOPPING. You aren't—you aren't going to sh-shoot him?

(*The* SUFFRAGETTE *relaxes and chuckles*)

SUFFRAGETTE. Good Heavens, no! We haven't got to that stage as yet, but I've no doubt it'll come, before they give us the vote.

TOPPING (*moving down* LC; *in awe*) Are you—one o' those—those Suffagettes?

SUFFRAGETTE. *Militant* Suffragettes, if you please. Yes, I'm one. And don't look at me as if I was a fiend from the Bottomless Pit. I'm just like you—two legs, two arms, one head—oh, there is one little different, I use mine in defence of my sex.

TOPPING (*astonished*) But you're—you're so young.

SUFFRAGETTE. Why shouldn't I be?

TOPPING. I thought they were all old and—and frumpish.

SUFFRAGETTE. Good heavens, how archaic. Don't you ever look at the newspapers?

TOPPING. No. I don't get the time. Besides, Mr Muspratt don't like me to.

SUFFRAGETTE. Who is Mr Muspratt, your husband?

TOPPING. Oh no, not yet. He's butler here. He an' me are practically steady.

SUFFRAGETTE. And you say he doesn't like you to read the newspapers?

TOPPING. No. He says they make young women coarse-minded.

SUFFRAGETTE (*outraged*) Good Heavens! Was there ever clearer proof of a male conspiracy to keep the whole lot of us in servile subjection? Don't you ever read them behind his back?

TOPPING. Oh no, I wouldn't do that, I believe in men knowing what's good for us.

(*This causes the* SUFFRAGETTE *acute pain*)
What is it? The stomach-ache?

SUFFRAGETTE. Heartache! Dreadful, agonizing heartache. I ought to get used to it but I never do, and I don't think I ever shall. How *can* one ignore the pitiful spectacle of five million slaves frenziedly kissing their fetters?

TOPPING. Jimminy, you 'ave got it bad, 'aven't you? (*She recollects her duty*) Here—how'd you get in?

SUFFRAGETTE. How should I? I climbed up the trelliswork.

TOPPING. Climbed up the . . . ? What for?

SUFFRAGETTE. Never you mind what for, just listen to me for a moment.

TOPPING. I'm not going to listen, I'm going to call the master before I get sacked. Climbed up the trellis. Whatever next! There's a front door, isn't there?

SUFFRAGETTE. I'm tired of knocking on it. Your employer happens to be one of our bitterest opponents.

TOPPING (*her courage returning*) And I don't wonder, neither—the way you carry on—chaining yourselves to railings, breaking shop windows, messing everything up with soot, flour and whatnot. My Prattie would have the whole lot of you transported if he was in Parlyment.

SUFFRAGETTE (*patiently*) Why is it that women like you are so much against us? You can call the police afterwards, but first please tell me why, I'm terribly curious.

TOPPING. Well—it's not just the things you do, it's the thing itself, I mean it's so daft. Votes for women, whoever heard o' such a thing—as if women needed laws to teach 'em how to get all they wanted out of a man.

SUFFRAGETTE. Don't they?

TOPPING (*warming*) Well, o' course they don't. Every woman's born with the ways an' means to manage a man properly.

SUFFRAGETTE. Yet you are not even allowed to glance at a newspaper.

TOPPING (*blankly*) What's that got to do with it? I don't *want* to glance at a newspaper. If I did I'd talk Muspratt into going out and buying 'em for me.

(*The* SUFFRAGETTE *is at ease now and* TOPPING'S *fear of her has quite evaporated*)

SUFFRAGETTE. This is terribly interesting. Am I to understand that by—by exercising your charms on Muspratt you could get him to agree to anything you asked?

TOPPING. Well, anything within reason, it's just a question of the right approach.

SUFFRAGETTE (*decisively*) Where is Muspratt at this moment?

TOPPING. Down in the kitchen having his supper. Why?

SUFFRAGETTE. Can you get at him?

TOPPING. 'Course I can get at him. That's why we had the speaking-tube fixed up.

SUFFRAGETTE. Speaking-tube?

TOPPING (*indicating the speaking-tube* R) There. It saves all our legs and speeds up the service.

SUFFRAGETTE. Tell me—what do you want most—most in the world—"within reason", as you say.

TOPPING. You mean, for myself like?

SUFFRAGETTE. Yes. Everyone of us has some secret longing for something—something that, with luck and hard trying we might be able to get.

TOPPING. Oh, I see. Well—there is something.

SUFFRAGETTE. What?

TOPPING. A bicycle.

SUFFRAGETTE. I beg your pardon?

TOPPING. A bicycle. Not just any bicycle but one o' them soft-tyred, three-speed "Elegants", like you see the Quality on Saturday afternoons. Look—(*she takes a folded advertisement from her apron pocket*) here it is, I cut this out to carry about with me. I look at it every so often to help pass the time.

SUFFRAGETTE (*glancing at the advertisement*) I see. Is your Mr Muspratt well paid?

TOPPING. Oh, he gets a wonderful "nominal"—half a sovereign a week. (*She replaces the advertisement in her pocket*)
SUFFRAGETTE (*horrified*) Good gracious! Do you mean to tell me that a butler to a Liberal Member of Parliament is only paid half a sovereign a week.
TOPPING (*blankly*) Aren't you funny? I said that's what his "nominal" was. He makes more than a lord in Parlyment on perks and tradesmen's bribes.
SUFFRAGETTE (*digesting this*) Oh, I see—then he's—er —he's relatively well off.
TOPPING. He's rolling in it.

(*The* SUFFRAGETTE'S *ignorance of what are, for* TOPPING, *the ordinary facts of life, has induced in her an open contempt for the intruder*)
You don't think I'd look at a man bald, and nearly fifty, if he wasn't, do you?
SUFFRAGETTE (*shocked*) Well, really, I must say . . .
TOPPING (*briskly*) Never mind what you must say. I can't stand here argufying, I got to see you're given in charge.
SUFFRAGETTE. No, wait—please—I was about to strike a bargain with you.
TOPPING. Bargain?
SUFFRAGETTE. Listen! You can hand me over, I know, but it'll mean trouble for you and your Muspratt.
TOPPING. How will it?
SUFFRAGETTE. Well, surely, it's part of your duties to keep people like me outside the main gates.
TOPPING (*not liking this*) Here, look here . . .
SUFFRAGETTE (*hastily*) I'll go quietly, I'll slip out of the same way as I came in, if you'll just do one little thing for me.
TOPPING (*suspiciously*) What?
SUFFRAGETTE. Prove something. Get Mr Muspratt on that speaking-tube, and ask him to give you a three-speed "Elegant" bicycle for your wedding present.
TOPPING (*astonished*) Well, I must say . . .
SUFFRAGETTE. Ah, then you were boasting, you know very well he'd flatly refuse you.

TOPPING. I don't know any such thing. As long as I play him off against young Mr Symonds, the groom, Mr Muspratt'd give me pretty near anything.

SUFFRAGETTE. All right, then, try him—but wait—if he refuses I stay here and listen to the speech.

TOPPING. Stay here! In this room!

SUFFRAGETTE. I'll never be noticed, with everyone coming and going. I'll probably be mistaken for one of the lady helpers. Well—are you sure enough of yourself to try?

(*The challenge appeals to* TOPPING *who wishes to demonstrate her power over Muspratt before an audience*)

TOPPING. I'll show you a better way to handle men than douse 'em with soot. (*She crosses confidently to the speaking-tube* R *and blows. In the conversation that follows she uses silken, persuasive tones*)

(*The* SUFFRAGETTE *sits on the settee.* MUSPRATT'S *replies come over the speaking-tube as a sonorous boom*)

(*Into the speaking-tube*) Is that you, Prattie, dear? . . . Oh, how *nice* to hear your voice . . . It's such a nice, deep, *manly voice* . . . (*She giggles*) Really, Prattie! You shouldn't say things like that over the tube, supposing any of the kitchen staff were to hear you? . . . Well, of *course* I will as soon as we've got rid o' the guests . . . Yes, I *know* there's a lovely moon, there was last night, wasn't there? . . . (*Coyly*) Well, that depends, Prattie. (*She turns aside to wink at the Suffragette*) I mean to say, it depends if I c'n be really sure you do love me . . . (*She giggles*) Tch! Tch! The things you do say, Prattie . . . Well, I *have* been thinking of you, but I've also been thinking of something else . . . No, I didn't say some*one* else—I said some*thing* else . . . Well, if you must know it's something nice, the something I want you to give me for a wedding present . . Oh, you'd never guess . . . (*She pauses between each word*) No . . . No . . . No . . . Wrong . . . Wrong . . . Wrong . . .

SUFFRAGETTE (*impatiently*) Oh, get on with it, do!

TOPPING (*to the Suffragette*) You can't rush this sort of

thing. You got to play 'em like a fish. (*Into the speaking-tube*) No... Then I'll tell you. Are you ready?... It's a bicycle... *A bicycle*... One of those latest soft-tyred, three-speed...

(*The faint rumbling on the tube suddenly swells to a roar*)

(*She holds the earpiece away from her and, from time to time, tries to check the flow*) Yes, but Prattie... No, but listen, Prattie... But I don't see why, Prattie...

(*The* SUFFRAGETTE *reacts gleefully to the storm*)

But, listen, dear... (*She puts her hand over the tube and turns beseechingly to the Suffragette*) Will a tandem do?

SUFFRAGETTE. Certainly not. The woman's seat of a tandem is the very symbol of her dependence on men.

TOPPING (*into the tube*) But, Prattie... Oh, but you must... But you've *got* to... But, listen I...

(*The sounds from the tube suddenly cease*)

(*She looks stupidly at the mouthpiece*) Prattie! Mr Muspratt! (*To the Suffragette*) He said all he'd got to say and then stuck the plug in at his end.

SUFFRAGETTE. I rather gathered he wasn't wholly in favour of the idea.

(TOPPING *crosses to* C. *Her expression is midway between bewilderment and annoyonce*)

TOPPING. He went off like a rocket. You'd have thought I'd asked for a private settlement.

SUFFRAGETTE. Oh, you'd have probably got that quite easily. You see—the law being what it is, any legal settlement of money on a woman isn't worth the tape it's tied up with.

TOPPING. But a bicycle. I mean—*everybody's* getting one—I've seen women riding them.

SUFFRAGETTE. You've seen *unattached* females riding them. Any married woman, or woman intending marriage, has the choice between the rear seat of a tandem or walking.

TOPPING. But why?

SUFFRAGETTE. It's just like I said, a man simply has to occupy the front seat of everything.
TOPPING. How do you become a suffragette?
SUFFRAGETTE (*rising and crossing to the table*) I can enrol you right now. (*She takes a reticule from the basket, opens it and extracts some leaflets, a notebook and a pencil*) Name?
TOPPING. Topping—Agnes, Amelia.
SUFFRAGETTE (*writing*) Age?
TOPPING. Twenty-one on June the first.
SUFFRAGETTE. Profession—housemaid. (*She hands some leaflets to Topping*)
TOPPING (*tartly*) *Parlour*maid. (*She takes the leaflets*) What are these for?
SUFFRAGETTE. To throw the moment the electors are let into the garden. You operate from a top-storey window, we don't want you sacked, you can be extremely useful to us in your present situation.

(IRIS FANSHAWE-SCOTT *enters* R. *She is a pretty, well-dressed girl of about twenty-two*)

IRIS (*as she enters*) Oh, Topping, I wonder if you'd . . . (*She sees the Suffragette*) I beg your pardon, are you one of daddy's lady canvassers?
TOPPING (*proudly*) No, she's a Suffragette.
IRIS (*shocked*) A *what*?
TOPPING. A Suffragette.
IRIS (*moving down* RC) What's she doing here?
TOPPING. She climbed up the trellis to get to the meeting. There's going to be real fireworks tonight isn't there, miss?
IRIS. But I—I don't understand. What are you doing with those leaflets, Topping?
TOPPING. Getting me instructions to throw 'em, Miss Iris.
IRIS. To throw them?
TOPPING. Yes, miss, the lady's just signed me on. (*To the Suffragette*) See if you can sign her on, she's got an awful lot to put up with, living on top of it, as you might say.

IRIS. Are you out of your senses? A Suffragette here, with daddy planning to speak from the balcony in there in less than half an hour? You'll be dismissed in the twinkling of an eye.

TOPPING. Oh, but I was leaving anyway, miss, I couldn't stay in the same place as Muspratt now this has happened.

IRIS. What has happened?

TOPPING. I've broken it off. I said he'd give me a bicycle and she said he wouldn't, and when I asked he said he'd as soon see me on a treadmill, miss, so I joined.

IRIS (*moving and sitting weakly on the chair down* R) Perhaps it's me that's imagining things. Pinch me, Topping, just make certain I'm awake.

SUFFRAGETTE. It's all perfectly simple. When I tried to explain to Topping what our movement stood for she said she knew how to manage any man, so I wagered her my presence here that she couldn't wheedle a bicycle out of Muspratt, and she couldn't. Aren't you Miss Iris Fanshawe-Scott?

IRIS. Yes—yes, I am.

SUFFRAGETTE. Then you must be the girl attached to that Tory-masquerading-as-Liberal, the Right Honourable Esmond Delahaye?

IRIS (*rising; angrily*) Don't you dare stigmatize Esmond as a Tory. He's daddy's secretary and my fiancé.

TOPPING (*corroborating*) That's right. They're engaged.

IRIS. And my father is bitterly opposed to Women's Suffrage, so it's not the slightest use you soliciting *his* support.

TOPPING. Oh, she didn't come here to do that.

IRIS. Then what did you come here to do?

SUFFRAGETTE. I came here to throw eggs at him.

IRIS (*faintly*) Eggs, you said?

SUFFRAGETTE. Certainly. (*She crosses to the table, takes an egg from the basket and displays it*)

IRIS (*moving to the table and examining the egg*) Why, they're Danish.

SUFFRAGETTE. Well, a Free Trader shouldn't mind that, should he?

IRIS. Topping! Summon the constable!

TOPPING (*sitting in the armchair up* LC *and folding her arms*) Not me, not after the lesson *I've* had.

(IRIS *makes a determined movement for the door* L, *but the* SUFFRAGETTE *gets there first and stands with her back to it*)

SUFFRAGETTE. One moment—why not give me the same chance that Topping gave me? You're opposed to us, I can see that, but it's only because your eyes have never been opened, it's only because you're ignorant of the sacrifice you'll make in marrying a reactionary like Delahaye.

IRIS. How dare you say that! What do you know of Esmond? He's not an ordinary politician, he's an idealist, a modern equivalent of Arthurian knighthood, a sweet, gentle, tolerant soul . . .

SUFFRAGETTE (*scornfully*) "*Tolerant*", you said. Why, when one of our members was gaoled for six months last week he wrote to *The Times* calling the sentence "preposterous leniency".

IRIS. He abhors violence, *any* violence. If you but knew it he's more than half-way persuaded you should be given the vote. Why, he told me only last night that our marriage was to be a partnership, that our home should be ruled as William and Mary ruled England, that I should be free to pursue any individual interest I might have.

SUFFRAGETTE (*puzzled*) He said that?

IRIS. In this very room, as we worked side by side on the crippled voters' lists.

SUFFRAGETTE. I'm delighted to hear it, I can't tell you how delighted, and if I could see it proved I should walk down to headquarters and hand in my badge on the instant.

IRIS (*checked*) You mean—if I demonstrated Esmond's breadth of mind to you, you would resign from the movement?

SUFFRAGETTE. Upon my honour.

TOPPING. Don't do it, Miss Iris, it's not half so yewmilly-atin' to take her on trust.

IRIS (*inspired*) Be silent, Topping. Do you imagine a sensitive spirit like Esmond's can be measured against a hidebound dummy like Muspratt? (*To the Suffragette*) How can I introduce you? What can I say?

SUFFRAGETTE (*equal to anything*) Say I'm a lady journalist—one of the truly emancipated, and that I've come here to request an interview on behalf of *The Woman's Sunday Companion*.

IRIS. An interview with him?

SUFFRAGETTE. Oh dear, no, with you—in search of the "distaff side" of a General Election. (*She moves down* L)

IRIS (*crossing to the door* L) Wait here. Topping, be handing the visitor refreshments. (*She knocks on the door and gently opens it*)

(*A rumble of voices is heard off* L. TOPPING *rises and crosses to the table* RC. *The* SUFFRAGETTE *crosses to the table* RC)

(*She peers off and calls gently*) Esmond—Esmond, my dear. Oh, forgive me for interrupting, Papa, but I must speak to Esmond, it's most urgent.

(ESMOND, *looking harrassed, enters* L *and stands by the door. He has some papers in his hand*)

ESMOND. What is it, my love?

IRIS. I want a word with you—in private.

(TOPPING *offers a sandwich to the Suffragette*)

ESMOND. Later, my dear. Your father and I are engaged in a last-minute check of his notes.

(IRIS *catches* ESMOND *by the arm, and ignoring his protests, closes the door and draws him to* LC)

But really, I must . . . (*He sees the Suffragette*) I beg your pardon. (*To Iris*) Who *is* this, my dear?

IRIS. Miss . . .

SUFFRAGETTE (*crossing to* C *promptly*) Quixley, special interviewer for the family magazine, the *Sunday Companion*.

(ESMOND'S *impatience vanishes. He becomes very suave, crosses to* L *of the Suffragette and shakes hands with her*)

B

Esmond. Oh, to be sure, a most excellent periodical. Very enterprising of you to call. (*To Iris*) You were perfectly correct to interrupt me, my dear, one must always *make* time for the Press. (*To the Suffragette*) I presume you wish to know Sir Hector's views on the Sabbath Observance Bill?

Iris. Oh, no, she wants a special interview, Esmond.

Esmond (*cordially*) Why certainly, certainly, but Sir Hector is terribly pressed for time just now. I think I could claim to answer any questions as he would wish them answered. Any particular issue—Home Rule, Free Trade, the Navy League . . .

Suffragette. No, Mr Delahaye, I'm after a much more original note, I was rather hoping I could interview your fiancée.

Esmond (*aghast*) My—my fiancée—Miss Fanshawe-Scott?

Iris. It's a wonderful idea, Esmond. She wants to tell her readers what it feels like to be a daughter to one possible Cabinet Minister and fiancée to a future Foreign Secretary. (*To the Suffragette*) You quoted a wonderfully apt title, Miss Quixley.

Suffragette. "The distaff side of a General Election."

Iris. That was it—a sort of up-to-the-minute survey of the part we women play in a General Election.

Esmond. Oh come, come, my dear . . .

Iris. But it's a wonderful idea—I mean—it would demonstrate that utter falsity of the Suffragette claim that, in all matters politic, women were herded into the background.

Esmond. On the contrary, I think it might well encourage them to continue to challenge us in the political arena. No, no, my dear, I couldn't possibly undertake to let you give an interview of that nature.

Iris. But, Esmond . . .

Suffragette (*cunningly*) You mean, sir, that if interviewed at all, Miss Fanshawe-Scott should confine herself to domestic matters.

Esmond. Precisely, but even with an article of that nature we should need time to prepare it.

SUFFRAGETTE. But we go to press in the early hours of tomorrow morning.
ESMOND. Then you could print it after the election. In any case, Sir Hector would certainly insist on vetting it.
IRIS. Vetting it! You mean—he—you—wouldn't even trust my discretion to make a statement on cookery and —needlework?
ESMOND (*easily*) Oh, it isn't a question of discretion, my darling, it's simply that your father and myself would have to ensure no statement you made could be mischievously torn from its context by our political opponents.
IRIS. But I've never heard of such a thing. I'm not a child, I'm . . .
ESMOND (*pompously*) Please, my dear. In this sort of sphere I must stress my superior judgement. I appreciate, of course, your praiseworthy enthusiasm . . .
IRIS. But, Esmond, you don't realize how terribly important your decision is.
ESMOND. Oh, but I do, my dear, of course it's important. That's why you should be guided by me in this delicate matter. (*To the Suffragette*) It was extremely civil of you to call, perhaps you could arrange with your editor to write for a second appointment next week? You will excuse me now, I'm sure.
IRIS (*clearly*) Esmond! Is that your final word?
ESMOND (*gently*) Yes, my love, it is. Now be a real help and assist Topping with the sandwiches.

(ESMOND *crosses and exits* L. IRIS *is in a cold but towering rage.* TOPPING *is resigned. The* SUFFRAGETTE *crosses to the table and gets her notebook*)

TOPPING. Well, you can't say I didn't warn you, can you, miss?
IRIS. "Sandwiches!" "Guided by him!" "Superior judgement!" Oh, it's insufferable.
SUFFRAGETTE (*making notes*) Name? Iris Fanshawe-Scott.
IRIS. Put "*Spinster*".
SUFFRAGETTE. Age?

IRIS. Twenty-one. Fully adult. Yet presumably incapable of expressing an opinion on crochet work!

(*The* SUFFRAGETTE *puts her notebook in the basket, takes the leaflets from Topping, halves them and returns one half to her*)

SUFFRAGETTE. I think we'll have enough to go round. (*She crosses and hands the remainder of the leaflets to Iris*) It might be as well if you threw them from here. (*She points to the balcony up* C)

IRIS (*taking the leaflets; uncomprehendingly*) When I reflect on his promises. He prattled for hours on equality of mind, sacred community of interests, the inviolable privacy of spirit . . .

SUFFRAGETTE (*casually*) I must lend you our Branch Chairman's pamphlet. It's called: *The Biggest Liars on Earth*. Now, ladies, if we could position ourselves for the attack. Topping, how good a shot are you with an egg?

TOPPING. Oh, I'm no good at throwing, miss.

SUFFRAGETTE. You aren't?

TOPPING. No, miss, the spirit's willing but the overarm's weak. I once threw a blancmange at Muspratt and missed him at three yards.

SUFFRAGETTE (*moving to the table*) Then perhaps you'd better take the soot, it has a more effective scattering range. How about you, Miss Fanshawe-Scott?

IRIS. Give me an egg. I was captain of netball.

(*The* SUFFRAGETTE *marshals her forces with a practised hand. She doles out a neat bag of soot to Topping and two eggs to Iris.*

LADY FANSHAWE-SCOTT, *unseen by the others, enters* R. *She is in evening dress, with spray. She is a pleasant, dignified woman, about fifty*)

SUFFRAGETTE. Now, the whole point of these ambushes is to create a situation in which calm speech——

(LADY FANSHAWE-SCOTT *stops short on catching the drift of the Suffragette's instructions.* IRIS *and* TOPPING *see her a second or so before the* SUFFRAGETTE *does, but are momentarily speechless with dismay*)

—even following the restoration of order, is quite impossible. The moment Sir Hector has said: "Ladies and Gentlemen," he begins to address his constituents through a thick coating of soot and egg yolk . . .
IRIS. Mother!
TOPPING. Madam!

(LADY FANSHAWE-SCOTT *is not alarmed but calmly sardonic*)

LADY FANSHAWE-SCOTT. Really, it's rather extravagant to use eggs, isn't it?
TOPPING. Oh, no, m'm, they're on'y imported.
LADY FANSHAWE-SCOTT. Oh, I see. That's rather different.

(*The* SUFFRAGETTE *looks helplessly to* IRIS *who does not fail her*)

IRIS (*recovering*) Come in and shut the door, Mummy.

(LADY FANSHAWE-SCOTT *closes the door and moves down* R)

(*To the Suffragette*) This is my mother, Miss Quixley and she'll be on the balcony. Don't you think, in the circumstances, we owe her a warning—you know, like the one Lord Mounteagle received from the Gunpowder Plotters?
LADY FANSHAWE-SCOTT. Perhaps someone would have the goodness to explain the nature of this extraordinary tête-à-tête.
IRIS. You're bound to know sooner or later, Mummy. Topping and I have joined the Suffragette Movement.
LADY FANSHAWE-SCOTT (*not as shocked as she might be*) Really? Am I to understand from that that your father has decided to sympathize with them?
TOPPING. Oh, no, m'm, it's him we're sooting and egging.

(LADY FANSHAWE-SCOTT, *having lived in an atmosphere of state affairs for some considerable time, is not overwhelmed by this, but merely shrugs*)

LADY FANSHAWE-SCOTT. Oh, then I follow you—this is a deliberately engineered attack to discredit the militants?

IRIS. Oh, no, Mother, we're serious, at least, I certainly am, after the terrible humiliation I have received from Esmond.

LADY FANSHAWE-SCOTT. What's Esmond been doing? Neglecting you?

SUFFRAGETTE (*feeling now that her ambush is out of the question*) It's a pity you came in when you did, Lady Fanshawe-Scott. (*To Iris*) I'm afraid there's nothing for it now but a strategic retreat. (*She collects the soot and eggs and replaces them in the basket*)

TOPPING (*disappointed*) Oh, no!

SUFFRAGETTE. I have strict orders not to embroil womenfolk in a militant action. You see, Your Ladyship, by demonstrating the inherent hypocrisy in the men of their choice I have succeeded, in less than an hour, in converting both your daughter and parlourmaid to the Cause. Now this, in itself, is a good evening's work, and I am more than content to leave it at that.

LADY FANSHAWE-SCOTT. Oh, come now, don't be so defeatist. Tell me, how were you able to convert them so rapidly and so wholeheartedly?

TOPPING. When I caught her in here she bet me I couldn't get Mr Muspratt to give me a bicycle for me wedding present.

IRIS. And she promised to leave here and abandon the movement if Esmond allowed me to give an uncensored interview to the *Sunday Companion*.

LADY FANSHAWE-SCOTT. And in both cases you were refused.

TOPPING. Muspratt said it was a tandem or nothing, m'm.

IRIS (*still smarting*) And Esmond said I must submit myself to his superior judgement. If he's as bigoted as that now, what will he be like when we're married?

LADY FANSHAWE-SCOTT (*to the Suffragette*) But precisely what were you trying to prove by these wagers?

SUFFRAGETTE. That no matter what promises were

made by the male before marriage, in all matters touching male vanity he takes refuge in automatically assuming superiority. That is the rock upon which our movement rests.

LADY FANSHAWE-SCOTT (*crossing and sitting on the settee*) I see. Well, as a matter of fact, I happen to be in a position to prove the contrary. If I hadn't been I might have been greatly impressed by your propaganda of late.

IRIS. Come now, Mother, be honest, you've never openly challenged Papa's authority in the whole of your married life.

LADY FANSHAWE-SCOTT. That's true, but I've never needed to. I have an income of my own.

SUFFRAGETTE. You mean you can spend how and what you like without reference to him?

LADY FANSHAWE-SCOTT. Not quite that, no. You see, when I was married the Women's Property Act had not even been amended. It was quite archaic, and consequently I made over my small fortune on marriage.

SUFFRAGETTE. And it has since reverted to you?

LADY FANSHAWE-SCOTT. No, it could do, but I've no occasion to revoke the original arrangements.

IRIS. You mean—technically—all your money is still father's.

LADY FANSHAWE-SCOTT. Of course.

IRIS. And you ask him for whatever you want?

LADY FANSHAWE-SCOTT. I draw an adequate allowance for housekeeping and personal expenditure.

SUFFRAGETTE. Submitting an account of your periodical needs, no doubt?

LADY FANSHAWE-SCOTT. Why, certainly. I make up the statement on the first of each month.

SUFFRAGETTE. Might I ask one further question, Your Ladyship?

LADY FANSHAWE-SCOTT. Certainly, and then, I'm afraid, I must have you shown out. I do hope you'll go without any fuss.

SUFFRAGETTE. I promise to—if you'll answer my question honestly.

LADY FANSHAWE-SCOTT. Well?

SUFFRAGETTE. Suppose—suppose you had occasion to demand—two hundred pounds—*now*—*tonight*. Would you get it?

LADY FANSHAWE-SCOTT. Not in gold, Sir Hector wouldn't have that much on him.

SUFFRAGETTE. But he'd have no hesitation in giving you a banker's draft?

LADY FANSHAWE-SCOTT. I don't think so—it's quite a big sum, but I've often demanded largish sums at irregular intervals.

SUFFRAGETTE. Stating, of course, the purpose for which they were required?

LADY FANSHAWE-SCOTT. Naturally.

SUFFRAGETTE. That's the point.

LADY FANSHAWE-SCOTT. I beg your pardon?

SUFFRAGETTE. I said, that's the point.

(TOPPING, *who has been following this catechism with open-mouthed interest, turns to Iris*)

TOPPING. What's she getting at now, miss?

IRIS (*tense*) I don't know. Shhh! Go on, Miss Quixley.

SUFFRAGETTE. As I was about to remark—you can get money—your *own* money, mark you—as often as you wish, but suppose the occasion arose when you preferred not to state the reason for which you wanted it? Would it be forthcoming under those circumstances?

(LADY FANSHAWE-SCOTT *is struck by this. She ponders*)

LADY FANSHAWE-SCOTT. Well, I really don't know. It's a very interesting point.

SUFFRAGETTE. Then I dare you to put it to the test.

LADY FANSHAWE-SCOTT (*intrigued*) What here? Now?

IRIS. Do it, Mother—oh, do it.

LADY FANSHAWE-SCOTT (*rising; determinedly*) Upon my soul, I think I will. Topping—your master certainly won't like to discuss such a matter in front of a parlourmaid, so be so good as to conceal yourself behind those curtains.

SUFFRAGETTE. Me, too? He might capitulate solely on

account of not wishing to appear close-fisted in front of a stranger.

LADY FANSHAWE-SCOTT. By all means, you've a good point there, but you can stay, Iris. Just knock on that door and summon your father. Tell him I've something extremely urgent to ask.

IRIS. But he's going over his speech with Esmond.

LADY FANSHAWE-SCOTT (*resolutely*) I don't care what he's doing. This is something that must be settled once and for all. Summon him.

(*The* SUFFRAGETTE *and* TOPPING *conceal themselves behind the curtains* R *and* L *of the window.* IRIS *crosses to the door* L *and knocks*)

SIR HECTOR (*off; testily*) What is it *now*?

(IRIS *opens the door a little*)

IRIS. Mummy wants to speak to you, Daddy. It's urgent.

(LADY FANSHAWE-SCOTT *moves down* RC, *turns, folds her arms and looks determinedly towards the door* L.

ESMOND *enters* L)

ESMOND (*to Iris*) Really, my pet, you are being rather trying—in less than ten minutes we're due to begin. (*He sees Lady Fanshawe-Scott*) I beg pardon, Your Ladyship, I'll—I'll tell Sir Hector.

(ESMOND *exits* L. *A mumble of voices is heard off.* IRIS *sits on the edge of the armchair* LC. LADY FANSHAWE-SCOTT *places two dining chairs facing one another* C, *and sits firmly in the one facing* L.

SIR HECTOR *bustles in* L. *He is vaguely irritated at being disturbed, but there is a certain latent respect in his general demeanour towards his aristocratic wife*)

SIR HECTOR (*crossing to* C) Really, my dear, I do feel that at a time like this I . . .

LADY FANSHAWE-SCOTT. Sit down, Hector.

SIR HECTOR. I've really no time, I . . .

LADY FANSHAWE-SCOTT. Sit down!

SIR HECTOR (*sitting on the chair facing her*) Is anything the matter, my dear?

LADY FANSHAWE-SCOTT. Perhaps not. We shall see.

SIR HECTOR (*glancing at his watch*) Then blow down the speaking-tube, Iris, and tell Muspratt to open the gates.

IRIS (*rising; dutifully*) Yes, Father. (*She crosses to the speaking-tube*)

SIR HECTOR. Now, my dear, whatever it is, please make haste.

LADY FANSHAWE-SCOTT. I want a banker's draft for two hundred pounds.

(SIR HECTOR's *incredulous gasp coincides with* IRIS's *warning whistle. The combination is comic*)

IRIS (*into the speaking-tube*) Open the gates, Muspratt. (*She replaces the whistle, crosses to the armchair, sits and folds her hands in her lap*)

SIR HECTOR (*finally*) Wh-what did you say?

LADY FANSHAWE-SCOTT. I said I wanted a banker's draft for two hundred pounds.

SIR HECTOR (*rising*) Well, really, my love, apart from the—the size of the amount, this is hardly the time to bother me with a housekeeping item.

LADY FANSHAWE-SCOTT. It isn't a housekeeping item, it's personal.

SIR HECTOR. Then it can wait until tomorrow.

LADY FANSHAWE-SCOTT. But it can't, Hector. I must have it this instant. Come now, your cheque-book is in your bureau drawer, I saw it there yesterday.

SIR HECTOR. But this is preposterous. (*With sudden alarm*) What would you want with such a sum?

LADY FANSHAWE-SCOTT. I refuse to tell you.

(*This causes* SIR HECTOR *to stagger a little and he decides to resume his seat*)

SIR HECTOR. I beg your pardon?

LADY FANSHAWE-SCOTT. I said I refuse to tell you.

SIR HECTOR. My love—are you ill?

LADY FANSHAWE-SCOTT. I was never better.

SIR HECTOR. But two hundred pounds—at such

notice, and without so much as a hint as to its purpose . . .

LADY FANSHAWE-SCOTT. Have you ever, in more than twenty-four years of married life, had occasion to doubt my judgement regarding money, my own, or yours, Hector?

SIR HECTOR. Certainly not, but . . .

LADY FANSHAWE-SCOTT. Have I ever landed you in debt, spent money recklessly, not accounted to you for every penny, even to my dress allowance and jewellery?

SIR HECTOR. No, but . . .

LADY FANSHAWE-SCOTT. Then give me that two hundred pounds this instant.

SIR HECTOR (*rising*) My dearest, I'll get Delahaye to send for Doctor Fotheringill.

LADY FANSHAWE-SCOTT (*rising*) I don't *want* Doctor Fotheringill. I want two hundred pounds.

SIR HECTOR. But you're ill—you must be.

LADY FANSHAWE-SCOTT. *I am not ill!* And in the whole of my life my brain was never so clear and so penetrating as it is at this instant. Are you going to give me that money?

SIR HECTOR. No! I most certainly am not.

(*Oddly enough this blunt statement calms* LADY FANSHAWE-SCOTT. *One feels her mounting anger has been merely a ruse. She resumes her seat*)

LADY FANSHAWE-SCOTT (*quietly*) Very well. You can go now, Hector.

SIR HECTOR. Go?

LADY FANSHAWE-SCOTT. Yes, that's all I wanted to know.

SIR HECTOR (*lamely*) You must promise me you'll go and lie down. Iris, ask one of the maids to . . .

IRIS (*rising*) Mother's perfectly well, Father—she's going to be with you at the meeting. You are, aren't you, Mummy?

LADY FANSHAWE-SCOTT (*grimly*) I wouldn't miss it for a king's ransom.

(ESMOND *enters* L. *A growing murmur from the crowd is heard off*)

ESMOND (*urgently*) They're beginning to get restless, Sir Hector. Perhaps I should open the windows.

SIR HECTOR (*vaguely*) Do, do by all means. I'll be with you in one second.

(ESMOND *exits* L)

Really, dear, I can't help feeling . . .

(LADY FANSHAWE-SCOTT *rises, crosses swiftly to Sir Hector and kisses him affectionately on his forehead*)

LADY FANSHAWE-SCOTT. There, there, Hector—don't distress yourself. We'll talk about it some other time, won't we, Iris?

IRIS. Yes, Mother. Lots of other times.

(SIR HECTOR, *only half reassured, exits* L. *The* SUFFRAGETTE *and* TOPPING *emerge from the curtains*)

LADY FANSHAWE-SCOTT (*turning to the table*) Young woman! Hand me that soot.

TOPPING (*moving hurriedly to the table*) Oh, no! She said *I* was to have the soot. (*She takes the bag of soot from the basket*)

LADY FANSHAWE-SCOTT. Topping! Have the goodness to hand me that soot this instant.

TOPPING (*hugging the bag*) No, no, it isn't fair—I joined before you did.

SUFFRAGETTE (*attempting to mediate*) Don't quarrel, please. There's plenty for everyone.

IRIS (*crossing to the table*) You have the flour, Mamma. There's two bags.

LADY FANSHAWE-SCOTT. I will *not* have the flour, I want the soot.

TOPPING. You shan't, it was promised to me.

(*Their voices rise in argument.*
ESMOND, *with a finger to his lips, enters* L)

LADY FANSHAWE-SCOTT (*to Topping*) You are in my house and you'll all act under my orders.

ESMOND. Please, Your Ladyship, Sir Hector is about to . . .

LADY FANSHAWE-SCOTT (*ignoring Esmond*) Young woman, you will advance from the left—Iris, you from the right—Topping, hold your bag in reserve until I give you the signal—I shall approach from behind . . . (*She takes a bag of flour from the basket*)

(*The* SUFFRAGETTE *takes a bag of flour from the basket and* IRIS *takes the eggs*)

ESMOND. Shh! I beg of you—Sir Hector is on the point of beginning.

LADY FANSHAWE-SCOTT. And so, young man, are we. Iris! Deal with Esmond.

IRIS. Certainly, Mother. (*She crosses to Esmond*)

(*A burst of applause is heard off*)

SIR HECTOR (*off*) Ladies and Gentlemen of my beloved constituency . . .

(IRIS *bursts the bag of flour over Esmond's head*)

LADY FANSHAWE-SCOTT. Forward by the right! Quick march!

In quasi-military formation the four WOMEN *advance, carrying their missiles towards the door* L *as—*

the CURTAIN *falls*

FURNITURE AND PROPERTY PLOT

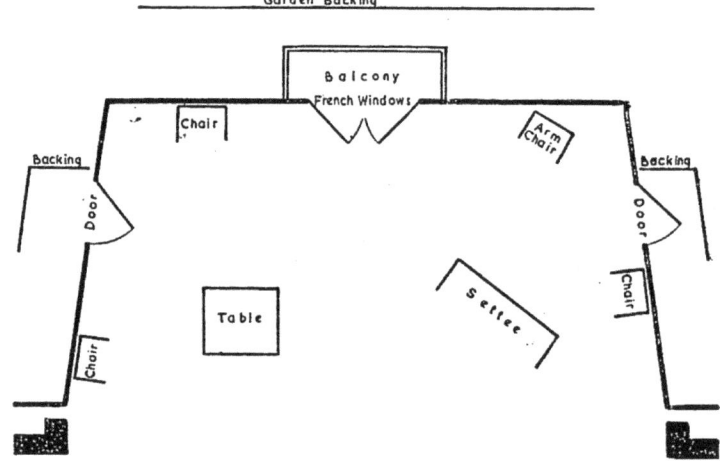

On stage: Table. *On it:* white cloth, small plates, knives, forks, entrée dishes with sandwiches, table-lamp
Settee. *On it:* cushions
Armchair
3 upright chairs
Heavy window curtains
Speaking-tube
Other period furnishings as desired

Off stage: Paper serviettes (TOPPING)
Basket. *In it:* reticule with leaflets and notebook, pencil, 2 eggs, bag of soot, 2 bags of flour (SUFFRAGETTE)
Papers (ESMOND)

Personal: ESMOND: notebook, pencil
SIR HECTOR: large watch
TOPPING: bicycle advertisement

LIGHTING PLOT

Property fittings required: table-lamp (practical)

Interior. The same scene throughout

THE MAIN ACTING AREAS are RC, C, up C and LC

THE APPARENT SOURCES OF LIGHT are french windows up C and a table-lamp RC

To open: effect of twilight
table-lamp lit

Cue 1   *At the rise of* CURTAIN *commence slow dim of off-stage lighting as darkness falls*

FILE COPY

PROPERTY OF
SAMUEL FRENCH LTD.